Beautiful BULBS

SIMPLE SECRETS FOR GLORIOUS GARDENS ⚜ INDOORS AND OUT

GEORGEANNE BRENNAN and MIMI LUEBBERMANN
photographs by FAITH ECHTERMEYER

CHRONICLE BOOKS
SAN FRANCISCO

❦ DEDICATED TO:
   EMME GILMAN (MCL)
   JIM SCHRUPP (GB)

ISBN 0-8118-4441-2

The Library of Congress has cataloged the previous edition as follows:
Brennan, Georgeanne, 1943-
Beautiful bulbs: simple secrets for glorious gardens—indoors and out/by
Georgeanne Brennan and Mimi Luebbermann; photography by Faith
Echtermeyer.
p.cm.
"A Garden Style Book."
Includes bibliographical references (p. 93)
ISBN 0-8118-0233-X (pb)
1. Bulbs. I. Luebbermann, Mimi. II. Title.
SB425.B65 1993
635.9'44-dc20
                                                92-27695
                                        CIP

Manufactured in China.

Design by Aufuldish & Warinner
Cover design by Tracy Sunrize Johnson

Distributed in Canada by Raincoast Books
9050 Shaughnessy Street
Vancouver, British Columbia V6P 6E5

10 9 8 7 6 5 4 3 2 1

Chronicle Books LLC
85 Second Street
San Francisco, California 94105

www.chroniclebooks.com

Contents

INTRODUCTION

Growing flowers from bulbs is simple and rewarding whether you are a novice or an experienced gardener. The mention of bulbs most often brings to mind spring flowers, such as bouquets of bright yellow daffodil blossoms, carpets of shining white spring snowflakes, and bunches of tulips, but there are also multitudes of bulbs that bloom in summer, fall, and winter.

¶Summer fills the garden with blooms of spiking gladioli, dahlia blossoms as big as barbecue plates, and arching stems of lilies. Tuberoses and Peruvian lilies planted in summer's full sun release their sweet, tropical fragrances into the warm air, while lushly succulent begonias make deep pools of brilliant color in the shade of lath houses and other sheltered gardens.

¶Atop naked stems, lavender and pink colchicum bloom in fall, ushering in the winter's season of indoor blooms. Bulbs can be forced to bloom ahead of their normal flowering season, in a technique by

which narcissus, hyacinth, huge amaryllis, and little grape hyacinth, among others, can give us color, fragrance, and pleasure during winter as well as in spring.

¶Succeeding with bulbs is easy because each bulb contains within itself the nutrients necessary for one full season of growth and bloom. The gardener provides light, water, and soil. Some bulbs, such as hyacinth, paper-whites, and amaryllis, don't even need the soil, and the colchicum can be forced to bloom inside without either soil or water.

¶We are so used to seeing photos in magazines and books of thousands of tulips, daffodils, or lilies growing massed along the streams of woodland estates or growing in drifts across an acre or so of lawn that it is easy to forget that bulbs can be grown in small spaces too. A container no larger than a teacup is large enough to grow a miniature daffodil, and a mason jar is just the right size for a hyacinth. A square foot or so of garden ground is transformed when planted with tulips or dahlias, and on a balcony or steps, tubs, and baskets can perch brimful with calla lilies or daffodils.

¶Although bulbs are virtually self-sufficient for a single, one-time show of bloom, and can be grown for a single season in almost any climate, it is quite a different matter to maintain bulbs for repeated bloom year after year. Some gardeners find that the one-time show of bloom satisfies their gardening impulse, and each year they again buy new bulbs to plant, discovering yet untried varieties and replanting old favorites. Other gardeners take pleasure from the nurturing and on-going preservation of their bulbs year after year, delighting in the process that brings the successful seasonal blooming.

¶In writing this book, as we discussed past experiences with bulb growing, our divergent passions became clear. Mimi loves the process of digging up the spent bulbs, whether container planted or planted in  the ground, letting them dry, then tenderly cleaning them for storage in carefully labeled bags until replanting time the following year. In winter, her house is filled with forced narcissus, amaryllis, and hyacinth, while her treasured dahlia and hybrid tulip bulbs are over-wintering safely in her cool, dry basement. Georgeanne, on the other hand, succumbed to the romance of the Turkish bulb breeders of the

Middle Ages, and to the vision of tiny tulips clinging to the rocky outcroppings of the Pamirs on the flanks of the Hindu Kush, and she grows species tulips for that reason — and for the fact that they naturalize and almost no effort is needed to maintain them. With the exception of her naturalized tulips and daffodils she treats bulbs as annuals, buying new ones every year, experimenting with different varieties, colors, shapes, and sizes. In spring, baskets full of tulips, daffodils, and hyacinths emblazon her front and back porches, while the first gladioli and begonias are putting up their shoots.

¶The practical purpose of this book is to offer an exploration of myriad options in variety, location, and growing methods of bulbs. There is a deeper purpose here, too. In this era of political upheaval, urban tensions, and a thousand daily irritations, the timed bloom of seasonal bulbs is a constant reassurance of the enduring pattern of nature. We hope that this book leads you toward discovery of your own interests and passions in the world of bulbs, and that you become as intrigued and soothed by their nature as we are.

A Cautionary Note

Please be sure you buy your bulbs from reputable dealers. There is an illegal trade in rare bulbs that is endangering the survival of some species. It is of gravest concern that we all only purchase bulbs from suppliers that are raising bulbs themselves, not stealing them from the wild.

CHARACTERISTICS OF BULBS

Bulbs" is the collective term for the bulbous species of plants that includes true bulbs, corms, tuberous roots, and rhizomes. In a wide sense, the bulbs' common characteristic is that each of them has the ability to store large amounts of food within special underground plant structures.

¶True bulbs are buds on a very, very short stem surrounded by closely packed leaves, called scales, in which food is stored. Hyacinths, narcissus, and lilies are examples of true bulbs.

¶Gladioli and crocuses are corms, which are actually stems swollen with food, with a bud on top. They produce side or lateral buds called cormlets.

¶When the root is the food storage organ, the dahlia being an example, the bulb is called a tuberous root and fibrous roots will develop from it.

¶A rhizome is a horizontal stem, usually just underground, that can swell with food and develop roots and also stems and leaves. Tuberoses are rhizomes.

THE CYCLE OF BULB GROWTH

The growth cycle of most bulbs is marked by several distinct phases. All bulbs have a dormant phase followed by a period of growth and flowering, then a period of food manufacture and storage.

¶During the dormant or nongrowing phases bulbs externally may appear to be at rest, but in fact there are numerous growth processes occurring on the inside.

¶In fall, as temperatures begin to drop in the outside garden, roots slowly begin to emerge from the bottom of the hardy bulbs, and the first sprouts poke barely out of the encircling layer of old scales yet remain hidden, underground. The bulb stays thus "dormant," slowly enlarging its root system, until spring temperatures begin to warm the ground. Then the sprouts elongate, extending up and through the earth, followed quickly by the flower stalk and then the flower itself. The energy for this growth comes primarily from the rapidly depleting food supply stored underground in the plant.

¶After flowering, the leaves' function is to produce sufficient food, stored underground, to fully provide for the next year's growth and bloom. When this is accomplished the leaves and roots wither and die naturally, as the bulb once again approaches dormancy.

¶The growth cycle for tender bulbs is similar but delayed into warmer weather.

¶By the time the leaves wither, the depleted bulb, the origin of this year's flower, has produced a new bulb or cormlet or has divided itself in some way, so that it has yielded to a new source of growth for the coming year. The result of this process happily often yields a number of new bulbs rather than just a single replacement for the spent bulb.

HARDY AND TENDER BULBS

"Hardiness" in bulbs is based on their ability to withstand the average minimum temperatures that occur, typically, during winter. Bulbs that originated in colder areas of the world can usually tolerate colder winters without damage, so they are referred to as hardy. They can be left in the ground year-round and treated as perennials. Hardy bulbs require a minimum period of cold during their dormancy or they will be unable to flower later. In warmer winter climates, hardy bulbs can't be left outside all year because they won't receive chilling sufficient to cause them to flower. They must be dug out of the ground and chilled artificially.

¶Nonhardy or "tender" bulbs generally are of tropical or semitropical origins and are not able to stand cold temperatures, so in colder climates they must be lifted, or dug, from the ground and kept inside during winter. In these conditions they are treated as annuals, being planted anew each year, although in their native climates they would be perennials.

About growing bulbs

The fact that bulbs are self-packaged growing units makes them vastly easier to grow than almost any other plant. Their ease notwithstanding, your meeting a few simple requirements can ensure the healthy growth of bulbs year after year. In all cases, you should start with top-quality bulbs, choosing the largest sizes offered.

¶Spring-flowering bulbs are planted in fall or winter. They are sold through catalogues mailed in June or earlier, but the bulbs don't appear in the nurseries until late summer. It is common for the mail-order houses to be sold out of spring-flowering bulbs as early as November. Summer- and fall-flowering bulbs are sold in catalogues mailed in December, and the bulbs appear in the nurseries about the same time. Some catalogue companies have only a single mailing that includes all their bulbs, but the orders are shipped in the appropriate season for planting.

¶The more unusual bulbs can often be found in specialty mail-order catalogues and in specialty nurseries. The largest varietal selections are found in catalogues that specialize in a particular kind of bulb.

Soil, Potting Mix, and Prepared Ground

Soil is a mixture of the three soil particles, sand, silt, and clay, plus any organic matter. Sand is chemically inactive, so it is the clay and silt and the organic matter that are involved in the complex exchanges of water and plant nutrients. Sand, however, is by far the largest in size of the particles, so the presence of sand means that there will be correspondingly large spaces between soil particles. These very large soil pores allow good drainage, favorable soil-atmosphere concentrations, and good horizontal water movement.

¶The organic matter in soils is old plant material, decomposing under constant attack by bacteria and fungi. Over time these liberate mineral elements that are essential to other plants for their growth.

¶An ideal soil would be composed of a mixture of sand, silt, clay, and organic matter in proportions that would allow good drainage and aeration yet have adequate water and nutrient-holding capabilities. A good loamy soil is about 60 percent sand, 20 percent silt, and 20 percent clay. Most soils are well under 5 percent organic matter. Commercial potting mixes are much, much higher in organic matter and much, much lower in sand. The addition of sand to these mixes greatly increases the ease of ensuring they receive adequate watering.

¶As adapted healthy bulbs reproduce themselves they take up more and more space in the soil. Consequently, higher percentages of sand and organic matter allow the bulbs to expand and multiply with less resistance than from a heavy, closely-packed soil. Furthermore greater amounts of sand and organic matter generally permit better drainage, which is critically important because most bulbs are susceptible to rotting in soggy conditions.

¶To prepare ground for planting, first remove existing plant material, such as weeds or plants you no longer want in the ground. With a shovel, a spade, or a machine, such as a rototiller, turn the soil over to a depth of 12 inches, adding sand and organic matter such as compost, rotted steer manure, or peat moss. Water once again and allow any undesirable seeds that may be in the ground to sprout. When the ground is dry enough to work, remove the newly germinated weeds. Using a hoe or shovel, break the soil up into small particles. The ground is now prepared for planting.

¶When planting the bulbs, generally follow the instructions given for planting depth, but for most, an inch or so either way is generally not critical. A rule of thumb is to plant the bulbs at a depth that is twice the height of the bulb. Using bulb planters or trowels or hoeing a trench all adequately serve the purpose of getting the bulbs to a proper depth, but it is important that the soil be firmly packed around each bulb so that water can move to it readily.

¶Interestingly, many bulbs have roots that contract to place themselves at a proper planting depth.

FERTILIZER

Generally commercial fertilizers list their content as the percentage of each nutrient, in the order nitrogen-phosphorus-potassium, so a 20-10-10 fertilizer would be 20 percent nitrogen, 10 percent each phosphorus and potassium. A balanced fertilizer contains about equal parts of each major nutrient.

¶Nitrogen is the nutrient used most heavily in green vegetative growth, and it may be a determining factor in the usage of other nutrients. Phosphorus and potassium are necessary for a wide range of plant functions especially during periods of rapid growth, but they are often linked to root and flower development.

¶Fertilizers come in many different forms, both dry and liquid. For most bulbs an all-purpose fertilizer adequately supplies nutrient needs, although for container plantings liquid fertilizers may be easier to apply.

¶During their initial growth and bloom, bulbs get their major nutrients from their own stored reserves. From the time of their emergence the leaves manufacture food, much of which is moved to the bulb and stored to use the next year. The plant's need for nutrients from fertilizer thus occurs primarily during and after bloom in this manufacturing period. Consequently the optimum time to fertilize is before bloom, so the nutrients are readily available to the plant when they are most needed.

WATER

Bulbs use water to transport nutrients and for photosynthesis, the energy-storing process. These are such fundamental requirements that water should always be available to the bulb and its roots, except during dormancy. A moist soil satisfies this condition but a soggy soil can induce rotting or restrict growth because the excess water fills the spaces between the soil particles, excluding oxygen and other desirable gases of the atmosphere. The amount of water needed by the bulb varies with its stage of growth, with greater amounts needed during periods of greater growth.

PESTS AND DISEASE

Bulbs are susceptible to an array of pests and diseases that vary by location. Obvious predators like moles, gophers, and mice can be readily detected, but very tiny insects, like bulb mites and thrips, are difficult to detect by those unfamiliar with their handi-work. There are various methods of control, and a local expert, like a nurseryman, should be able to make informed suggestions for the most apt solution in your location.

LIFTING AND STORAGE

In colder regions, tender, summer-flowering bulbs need to be dug or "lifted" from the ground and stored where they won't freeze.

¶When the tops have died back, or after the first frost, carefully dig the bulbs and shake the soil from them. Let them dry for a few days, then put them in labeled paper bags or in boxes and store them inside at about 65 degrees in a dry place.

Tender bulbs in their containers can be left dry in their containers and moved to an area protected from freezing.

¶In warmer regions hardy bulbs should be lifted after the tops have died back and stored at about 65 degrees. To induce next year's flowering, the bulbs should then have a storage period of 8 to 10 weeks at a temperature slightly less than 48 degrees.

¶Unlike tender bulbs, the hardy bulbs are best stored in a slightly humid environment.

BULBS to
FORCE
INSIDE

orcing bulbs is one of the simplest and most rewarding ways to bring masses of bright blooms into your house, especially in winter. The cold dark winter days invite bringing containers of brightly colored flowers, often sweetly scented, into every room. ❧ To force bulbs to grow and flower indoors during winter, it is necessary to simulate their normal outdoor growth cycle but expose them to warmth sooner than they would have been naturally. ❧ In general, dormant bulbs should be potted, watered, then placed in a cool (40 degree to 50 degree) dark location for eight to twelve weeks, allowing their roots to develop. After the roots have developed and there are sprouts about 2 inches tall, the pots should be moved to a semidark area for a week, then to a warmer area (55 to 65 degrees) with full light but no direct sunlight. When the sprouts are about 6 inches tall and ready to bloom the pots should be moved into direct sunlight in a cool spot until the flower buds begin to show color. ❧ Once they begin to bloom, flowering can be prolonged by avoiding both full sunlight and warmer temperatures. At all stages of forcing the soil should be kept moist. ❧ Some bulbs, notably the tender narcissus and amaryllis, can be forced directly, without needing to go into a dark location. ❧ Narcissus, amaryllis, and hyacinths can be forced to bloom in water alone, with or without fillers such as marbles, pebbles, or seashells. The roots grow around the filler, serving to anchor the bulb and its eventual flower stalk. When bulbs are forced in water with or without filler, it is essential to keep the bulbs just above water level, with only the roots touching the water. Bulbs will rot if left to stand in water. ❧ Most bulbs that have been forced, disrupted from their natural cycle, are then discarded, because they do not produce good blooms again for a couple of seasons, even with the best of care.

AMARYLLIS

Amaryllis bulbs seem ebullient in their enthusiasm to bloom, and with good reason. Of tropical origins, amaryllis bloom naturally in winter and, in spite of their exotic, other-worldly appearance, they are one of the easiest of all bulbs to grow indoors, needing only warmth and water. ¶ The intrepid Dutch bulb breeders have bred seductive varieties of hybrid amaryllis as high as three feet tall with nine-inch trumpetlike blooms in all colors — pink, white, red, salmon, striped, and spotted — that will grow and bloom indoors from October until February, or even into March. Amaryllis bulbs potted the last week of October through mid-November will be in full splendor in time for the December holidays. ¶ Amaryllis have such heavy heads, usually bearing three to four huge flowers each, that sometimes even their thick strong stalks can't keep them from toppling over. To give the stalks added support, if you are growing them in a container with potting mix, tie them to a stake to prop up the top-heavy flowers. (If you are growing amaryllis in water alone, choose tall containers with narrow necks long enough to hold the blooms upright.) ¶ Because amaryllis grow so large so quickly and easily, they make a particularly suitable garden project for children, as well as the rest of us who respond to almost-instant gratification. ¶ **HOW TO DO IT** ¶ For one amaryllis bulb, choose a container 6 inches wide and 8 to 10 inches deep with a hole in the bottom. Cover the bottom of the container with a layer of pebbles, gravel, or bits of broken pottery. Fill it half-full with moist potting mix. Place the bulb, root side down, pointed tip upward, on top of the mix

Hybrid Amaryllis

Hippeastrum hybrid

12 to 36 inches high

White, red, salmon, pink, or variegated

What You Need

1 bulb

Container 6 inches in diameter and
8 to 10 inches deep

Gravel, pebbles, or bits of broken pottery

Potting mix

When to Buy

June through January from
catalogues; late summer through early
spring from nurseries

When to Force

October through February

When Blooms Appear

6 to 8 weeks after planting

so that the upper one-third of the bulb is exposed above the rim. Fill in the space between bulb and container. Water thoroughly, allowing the potting mix to become saturated. ¶ Place in a warm location and keep the soil slightly moist but not soggy until the first growth appears, then move the container to a sunny location, maintaining the moisture until the amaryllis blooms. To prolong the bloom, move the plant out of the direct sunlight.

AUTUMN CROCUSES

Autumn crocus might be called the miracle bloomer of the bulb world, because from the leathery bulb will emerge pale, twisting stems unassisted by either soil or water. Within a week or so thereafter, vase-shaped flowers appear and then slowly open. When grouped closely together on a piece of glass or a plate, or in a shallow bowl, the growing stems and flowers of the bulbs will twist and curl, interlocking with and overlapping one another to form a naturally stylized arrangement. ¶ Because autumn crocuses are dormant only for a short period in late summer, and start to bloom immediately thereafter, only this small window of time is available for acquiring these extraordinary bulbs. ¶ Autumn "crocus" is, in fact, not a crocus at all, but a colchicum. Numerous types exist in colors ranging from purple and deep pink to iridescent pink and white. ¶ **HOW TO DO IT** ¶ For twelve to fifteen bulbs you will need a plate, shallow bowl, or other flat or semi-flat surface about 12 inches in diameter or square. Put the bulbs close together, even stacked on top of each other, and sprinkle with water if desired. Keep the plate or bowl in indirect light.

Autumn Crocus
Colchicum autumnale, C. speciosum

❧

6 to 8 inches high
Pinks, purples, or white

❧

What You Need
12 to 15 bulbs
Plate, shallow bowl, or other flat
or semiflat surface about
12 inches in diameter

❧

When to Buy
Order as soon as possible from
spring and summer catalogues; in July
from most nurseries

❧

When to Force
As soon as bulbs are available

❧

When Blooms Appear
3 to 6 weeks after planting

❧

GRAPE HYACINTH

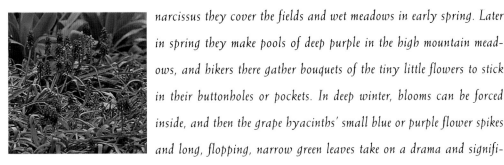

Grape hyacinths are natives of the Mediterranean region, where along with the first narcissus they cover the fields and wet meadows in early spring. Later in spring they make pools of deep purple in the high mountain meadows, and hikers there gather bouquets of the tiny little flowers to stick in their buttonholes or pockets. In deep winter, blooms can be forced inside, and then the grape hyacinths' small blue or purple flower spikes and long, flopping, narrow green leaves take on a drama and significance out of proportion to their size. ¶ Grape hyacinth bulbs can be purchased in late summer and early fall, and if potted in late October, will be blooming in January or February. Several different varieties are available, including a white form. ¶ **HOW TO DO IT** ¶ For twelve to eighteen bulbs, choose a container 6 inches in diameter and 8 to 10 inches deep with a hole in the bottom. Cover the hole with a little gravel, a few small rocks, or bits of broken pottery. Add moist potting mix to within 3 inches of the rim. Place the bulbs about 1 inch apart, root side down and pointed tip upward. ¶ Cover the bulbs with moist potting mix to within 1 inch of the rim. ¶ Place the container in a cool dark place for three to four weeks to allow root development to begin, watering about once a week. ¶ Bring the container out of the dark and place it in a cool, light location. Keep the potting mix moist during growth and bloom.

Grape Hyacinth

Muscari

❦

6 to 9 inches tall

Deep rich purple, blue, or white

❦

What You Need

12 to 18 bulbs

Container 6 inches in diameter and
8 to 10 inches deep

Gravel, small pebbles, or bits
of broken pottery

Potting mix

❦

When to Buy

Summer and fall from catalogues;
in fall from nurseries

❦

When to Force

October through February

❦

When Blooms Appear

3 to 4 months after planting

❦

Hyacinth

Hyacinths are such a popular bulb for forcing that special forcing glasses were designed as long ago as the eighteenth century. The glasses were created in different shapes, but many of them resembled the wide-based towers of medieval castles topped with ruffled or straight-sided parapets. Other glasses were bulbous or shaped like Grecian urns, but all of them had narrow necks to cradle the bulb while the dangling roots swirled in the water in the base. ¶ Often dozens of hyacinths, forced in various glasses of red, blue, green, amber, and gold, lined the shelves and filled the tables of nineteenth-century parlors and drawing rooms. However, only three or four blooming hyacinth stalks are necessary to fill a room with their fragrance. ¶ A hyacinth can certainly be forced in an ordinary jar, vase, or other container as long as the bulb's base just barely touches the water. It can also be forced in soil, but seeing the roots curl and twist in the water is one of the charms of the forced hyacinth. ¶ **HOW TO DO IT** ¶ For one hyacinth bulb, choose a glass jar, vase, or other container at least 4 inches tall and with a neck narrow enough to hold the bulb suspended. Fill the container with water to reach just to the bottom of the bulb. Add filler, such as pebbles or marbles if you wish. Place the bulb in the neck, and then store the container in a cool dark place for three to four weeks to allow the roots to begin developing. Maintain the water level while the roots are developing. ¶ When roots are at least 2 inches long and leaves have sprouted, bring the container out into a location with bright indirect light. Maintain the water level for the life of the plant. When the leaves have turned green, place the container in a location that gets direct sun, rotating it periodically to encourage upright growth. When bloom occurs, again move the container, avoiding direct sunlight to prolong the bloom.

Hyacinth

Hyacinthus orientalis

❧

8 to 10 inches tall

Shades of white, pink, salmon, and blue

❧

What You Need

1 bulb per container

1 container, a traditional hyacinth forcing glass or other

Pebbles, marbles, or other filler (optional)

❧

When to Buy

June through December from mail-order catalogues;

August through December from nurseries

❧

When to Force

October through March

❧

When Blooms Appear

10 to 12 weeks after planting

❧

NARCISSUS

The clean, spicy fragrance of blooms of forced narcissus hangs gently on the air and, no matter how many are flowering at one time, it never seems overpowering. The most commonly forced narcissus is called 'Paper-white,' a variety with pure white cups and petals, but the old-time favorite narcissus for forcing was 'Chinese Sacred Lily,' which has pale yellow petals, a golden orange cup, and a sweet perfume. 'Grand Soleil d'Or' is an old favorite as well, and it is entirely yellow. ¶ By October, narcissus bulbs are available and can be kept stored in the refrigerator or another cold place until time to plant. When planted in October, November, and December the bulbs will take several weeks before they bloom, but in January, February, and March, as the bulbs approach their natural flowering time, the days from planting to bloom may shorten to ten to twelve. ¶ **HOW TO DO IT** ¶ For six to twelve bulbs you will need a bowl, shallow tray, vase, or other container at least 6 inches in diameter and 3 to 4 inches deep. The simplest way to force the narcissus listed above is in water, along with marbles, pebbles, or other non-nutritive filler. ¶ The roots wrap around and through the filler, stabilizing and anchoring the bulb, and thus provide support for the flowering stalks. ¶ After putting at least 2 inches of filler in the container, place the bulbs on it, root sides down and pointed tips upward. Add additional filler around the base of each bulb, leaving about three-quarters of the bulbs' surface exposed. ¶ Fill the container with water just to the base of the bulbs. Maintain the water level throughout the life of the plant. For best root development, put the planted container in a cool spot away from the light for about two weeks, then move the container into a bright location. Green stalks will appear, followed shortly by blooms. Rotate the container periodically to encourage upright growth. If a stalk threatens to fall over, tie it to a stake.

Narcissus, Chinese Sacred Lily

Narcissus tazetta, N. tazetta
var. orientalis

❧

12 to 16 inches tall
White, yellow, or white and orange

❧

What You Need
6 to 8 bulbs, 'Paper-whites,'
'Cragford,' 'Grand Soleil d'Or,'
'Chinese Sacred Lily'
Container at least 6 inches in diameter
and at least 3 or 4 inches deep
Marbles, pebbles, clean sand, or
other filler

❧

When to Buy
June through October from catalogues;
September through January from nurseries

❧

When to Force
October through March

❧

When Blooms Appear
3 to 4 weeks after planting

❧

BULBS TO
GROW IN
CONTAINERS

Almost every gardener has a reason for growing at least some bulbs in containers. Containers are mobile, so they are easily transported from one place that's optimum for growth to another where the growing bulbs can be sheltered. As an alternative to growing in the ground, growing in containers is an important consideration where space is limited or unavailable. ❧ Planted in containers, flowering daffodils and other bulbs that are susceptible to wind and rain damage can be moved out of the path of storms that tear the blossoms and level the plants. Bulbs such as calla lilies that are not frost hardy can be moved to protected areas when they are container planted, to reduce the risk of frost injury. ❧ Most importantly, containers provide a full range of gardening experiences and pleasure for people who do not have ground or who are unable to get down on their hands and knees and dig and turn the earth, pull the weeds, and otherwise tend to the caretaking of a garden. ❧ Almost all bulbs can be planted in containers and grown for a single season, and some, such as freesias and calla lilies, can be maintained in the same container year after year. Begonia and tulip bulbs, on the other hand, do not adapt well to overwintering year after year in the same container, and when their blooming season is over should be lifted, dried, and stored, and then replanted the next season. ❧ When bulbs are planted in containers, good drainage is a necessity for successful growth and flowering. Soggy, wet, undrained soil will result in rotted bulbs and disappointed gardeners.

CYCLAMEN

At least once a year, perhaps, there comes a time when we are all overcome by the desire to have a container abundant with beautiful flowers growing in our houses — right that minute. This is quite a different emotion from the reasoned one that sends us forth in fall to nurseries, that makes us thumb through the pages of mail-order catalogues to order bulbs that won't bloom for months. The latter impulse is about process and planning and rewards for labors well performed. The longing for an already-grown, already-beautiful plant is about the immediate enjoyment of beauty. When that longing arises, go to a nursery or garden center and buy a cyclamen already in leaf and bloom. ¶ Although cyclamens can readily be grown from bulbs by the home gardener, the cheerful, colorful plants are so widely available in bloom from September through February that it seems worth taking a shortcut. Cyclamen come in a variety of colors and forms, from dark reds to light pinks, with frilled petals or smooth ones, and in miniature as well as full-sized types. They will bloom inside or outside in mild climates over a three-month period if kept watered and fertilized. ¶ **HOW TO DO IT** ¶ Choose a plant in a 6- or 8-inch pot. Check under the leaves and verify that there are new blossoms just starting, to guarantee a long period of bloom. At home, slip the container into a decorative cachepot, if desired. ¶ Keep the plant inside in a cool location that receives a few hours of direct sun. Keep the potting mix barely moist, but not wet, for continued blooming. Remove spent blooms and dead leaves by gently pinching their stalks off at the base of the bulb. Fertilize once a month with a liquid fertilizer.

Cyclamen

Cyclamen persicum

❧

4 to 12 inches tall

White, pink, red, or variegated

❧

What You Need

1 potted plant

Cachepot (optional)

Liquid fertilizer

❧

When to Buy

September through February from nurseries, garden centers, and florists

❧

When Blooms Appear

Before purchase

❧

Double-layered Daffodils

Double layers of daffodil bulbs packed snugly together in a basket, pot, or other container will, upon blooming, burst into a near-solid mass of color. When the bulbs are planted in two layers, the gaps between bulbs and the subsequent open spaces between flowers are filled, and the sought-after effect of superabundance is achieved even by the extreme novice. The admirable final result of your efforts will make you feel like a seasoned floral designer. ¶ 'King Alfred,' a reliable old-fashioned variety with large, bright yellow cups, was once the standard, but now there are dozens and dozens of different varieties of daffodils with double trumpets, frilled edges, multiple blooms, short cups, and long cups, all available in salmon, pink, cream, yellow, and various mixtures thereof. All of them, including the miniature types, will be successful and quite beautiful when grown in containers. ¶ **HOW TO DO IT** ¶ For a massed planting of thirty to thirty-five bulbs, choose a container at least 18 inches in diameter and 12 to 18 inches deep with a hole in the bottom. Cover the bottom of the container with a layer of gravel, small pebbles, or bits of broken pottery. ¶ Fill the container with a 4- to 6-inch layer of potting mix. Place about twenty of the bulbs, root sides down, pointed tips upward, on top of the mix in a single layer. They should almost be touching one another. Make a second layer with the remaining bulbs offset on top of the first layer. Cover with potting mix to within 1 inch of the rim, and soak with water. ¶ In mild climates, keep the container outside, or in cold climates, inside in a cool, dark place. Keep potting mix moist from the time of planting until end of bloom. If the bulbs are kept inside, once 2 inches of sprouts show, bring the container into the light.

Daffodil

Narcissus

4 to 16 inches tall

Yellow, white, salmon, or multicolored

What You Need

30 to 35 bulbs

Container at least 18 inches in diameter

and 12 to 18 inches deep

Gravel, small pebbles, or bits

of broken pottery

Potting mix

When to Buy

July through November from

mail-order catalogues;

August through November

from nurseries

When Blooms Appear

3 months after planting

EARLY TULIPS

The description "tulip shaped" still indicates the elongated cup or smooth chalice of the classic tulip. However, tulips are now available with petals in many fanciful shapes, from wild, splaying, and fringed to geometrically pointed to fat, thick petals wrapping around themselves in so many layers that the flower looks like a peony rather than a tulip. These are mostly hybrids, and they come in almost every hue. ¶ Not all tulip varieties bloom at the same time. You will notice, particularly when purchasing bulbs from mail-order catalogues, that some tulips are labeled early, others midseason, and still others late blooming. Most of the early bloomers are those with relatively short stems and the regular "tulip" shape, while the more unusual ones tend to be late bloomers. For bloom in February and March, choose tulips labeled single early, double early, or kaufmanniana species or hybrids. All tulips bloom better if they undergo a period of chilling. Unless you are sure your bulbs have been precooled, store them in your refrigerator for a month or more before planting them. ¶ **HOW TO DO IT** ¶ For twenty-four bulbs, choose a container 18 inches in diameter and at least 18 inches deep with a hole in the bottom. Cover the hole with a little gravel, a few small rocks, or bits of broken pottery. Fill the container with potting mix to within 4 inches of the rim. Place the bulbs closely together, almost touching, on the mix, root sides down and pointed tips upward, and fill the container to within 1 inch of the rim with potting mix. Water to thoroughly saturate the mix. Keep the potting mix moist until bloom has finished. ¶ In cold climates, keep the planted containers in a cool dark place until bulbs begin root development and 2 inches of sprouts show, and then move the container to a protected location that has at least a half-day of direct sun. In mild climates the containers can stay outdoors.

Tulip

Tulipa

❧

5 to 14 inches tall (single early, double early, kaufmanniana)
White, pinks, reds, yellows, purples, or variegated

¶

What You Need
24 early-flowering bulbs
Container at least 18 inches in diameter and 18 inches deep
Gravel, small rocks, or bits of broken pottery
Potting mix

❧

When to Buy
August through December from mail-order catalogues; September through January from nurseries

❧

When to Plant
October through November

❧

When Blooms Appear
February through March

❧

Freesias

A sweet, clean, faintly citrus fragrance surrounds the small blossoms that festoon each thin, reedy freesia stem. Freesias come in many colors, including soft pastels of pink, lavender, and white and sharp bright shades of red, purple, and yellow. ¶ At first glance, though, even the brightly colored ones seem unprepossessing, and you might question whether it is worth the time and effort to grow them, especially in comparison with glamour bulbs like amaryllis and tulips. The freesia's beauty lies not in flamboyance, however, but in its graceful arching shape and delicate fragrance. ¶ Freesias grow well in containers indoors as long as nighttime temperatures are cold, but they will not grow and bloom successfully in overheated rooms or near radiators or other heat sources. They may be grown outdoors in containers in mild winter areas. ¶ **HOW TO DO IT** ¶ For six bulbs, choose a container 6 inches in diameter and at least 8 inches deep with a hole in the bottom. Cover the hole with a little gravel, a few small rocks, or bits of broken pottery. ¶ Fill the container to within 4 inches of the rim with moist potting mix. Place the bulbs 2 inches apart, root side down, pointed tips upward, on the surface of the mix. Cover with moist potting mix to within 1 inch of the rim. ¶ Keep the container in a sunny location but where nighttime temperatures are cool. Keep potting mix moist but not soggy. After the bulbs have sprouted, fertilize monthly with a dilute solution of liquid fertilizer. If flower stalks threaten to fall over, tie them to stakes. ¶ Freesias may be left in the same container for several years, or they may be lifted and stored and then replanted each year. When bloom ends, reduce watering, allowing the foliage to yellow and wither. Start watering again in the fall.

Ranunculus

The ranunculus is the true Cinderella among the bulbs. Like the fairy tale's classic transformation of the ugly to the beautiful, showy crepe-petaled blooms will sprout from a wizened, many-legged bulb. Grown in pots, these bulbs are a flower factory, reliably presenting dazzling ready-made bouquets of full-flowered blossoms. ¶ Over the last thirty to forty years, a glamorous strain of ranunculus called Tecolate has been developed that has cupped petals, layer after layer, resembling the inward-folding flowers of old-fashioned roses or camellias. The flowers are large and the petals stay on considerably longer than those of the unimproved strains which tend to blow off with the first strong breeze. ¶ Ranunculus can also be bought in nurseries already in leaf, to be transplanted into your containers, allowing you to not miss the chance to have ranunculus even if you missed the bulb-buying and planting season. ¶ **HOW TO DO IT** ¶ For fifteen to twenty bulbs, choose a container at least 12 inches in diameter and 12 to 18 inches deep with a hole in the bottom. Cover the hole with a little gravel, a few small rocks, or bits of broken pottery. ¶ Fill the container to within 4 inches of the rim with potting mix. Gently push the pointed ends of the bulbs into the mix, spacing them about 2 inches apart, and cover with a 2-inch layer of potting mix. Water thoroughly, until the potting mix is soaked. ¶ Keep the container in a frost-free location in full sun. Keep the mix only slightly moist, because the bulbs are prone to rotting if they are in soggy conditions.

Ranunculus

R. asiaticus

❧

10 to 16 inches tall

Red, yellow, pink, white,

salmon, or orange

❧

What You Need

15 to 20 bulbs

Container at least 12 inches in diameter

and 12 to 18 inches deep

Gravel, small rocks, or bits

of broken pottery

Potting mix

❧

When to Buy

July through November from

mail-order catalogues;

August through November

from nurseries

❧

When to Plant

September through December

❧

When Blooms Appear

3 to 4 months after planting

❧

TUBEROUS BEGONIA

Full-flowered begonia blossoms bring to mind swirls of fluorescent crinolines and petticoats, twirling on a warm summer night. The succulent leaves and full velvety petals of the tuberous begonias become sensual clumps of color when potted and put on a balcony or tucked into the niche of a garden wall. Although the plant is dominated by its big, multilayered male flowers, each plant has small, female blossoms as well. ¶ There are numerous fascinating species of begonia, but the tuberous begonia of the garden and lath house is a hybrid, bred from several different species native to the Andes. The exotic appearance of the tuberous begonia belies the ease with which it can be grown in all but the hottest areas; and even in hot areas, provided with rich soil, lots of shade, and misting water, it can be grown successfully. ¶ **HOW TO DO IT** ¶ For a single 2-inch size begonia bulb, either an upright type or a cascading type, choose a container 8 inches in diameter and 10 inches deep. ¶ Make sure your container has a drainage hole in the bottom. Cover the hole with a little gravel, a few small rocks, or bits of broken pottery. ¶ Fill the container with potting mix to within 2 inches of the rim. Place the bulb in the center of the container, rounded side facing down. If you see pink tips on your bulb, these are the budding sprouts, not roots, so these sprouts should be facing upward. Add enough potting mix to come up the sides of the bulbs but leave the tops uncovered. Water thoroughly, until the mix is saturated. In cold climates, keep the container inside in a location with a half-day of direct sun, and after all danger of frost has passed, move it outside to a location with a half-day of filtered sun. ¶ Once two leaves have appeared, fertilize every two weeks with a complete liquid fertilizer diluted to half-strength until the bloom has finished. ¶ Keep the potting mix moist at all times but not soggy, as tuberous begonias are susceptible to powdery mildew, which is a fungal growth on the leaves generally caused by overly wet soil.

WHITE CALLA LILIES

Both the flowers and the big, heart-shaped leaves of white calla lilies have a sinuous flip and curl to their edges that appealed to designers and artists of the art deco period. The plant's form, either entire or in part, was recreated endlessly on brass lamps, sterling silver flatware, posters, and even on lace curtains of the era. ¶ To see a dozen or more white calla lilies grown to maturity massed together in a container, their shapes a ripple of curving lines, can cause one to understand the designers' fascination with this plant's patterns. Snipped from the container and brought into the house to use as a cut flower, the calla will keep for days with its beauty undiminished. ¶ White callas produce lush foliage and flowers when grown in containers filled with a rich soil mix, and when kept fertilized they stay green, producing blooms year-round in cool, mild climates. In areas where temperatures drop below freezing, however, the plants, when in containers, must be overwintered inside, or the bulbs be dug after blooming and stored for replanting the following spring. ¶ In addition to the classic white calla, colored varieties and a dwarf white are also available, and they may be grown in the same way as the large white calla. ¶ **HOW TO DO IT** ¶ For six to eight calla lily bulbs, choose a container at least 18 inches in diameter and 12 inches or more deep with a hole in the bottom. Cover the bottom of the container with a layer of gravel, pebbles, or bits of broken pottery. Fill with moist potting mix to within 3 inches of the rim. Place the ✦

White Calla Lily

Zantedeschia aethiopica

❧

2 to 4 feet tall

❧

What You Need

6 to 8 bulbs

Container at least 18 inches in diameter and at least 12 inches deep

Gravel, small pebbles, or bits of broken pottery

Potting mix

Liquid fertilizer

❧

When to Buy

June through March from mail-order catalogues;

September through February from nurseries

❧

When to Plant

Fall in mild climates; spring elsewhere

❧

When Blooms Appear

Mid-spring to early summer

❧

bulbs 3 inches apart and 3 inches in from the rim. Cover the bulbs with moist potting mix to within 1 inch of the rim, and put the container in a location, indoors or out, that receives only a half-day of direct sun, preferably morning sun. ¶ Keep the potting mix moist, but not soggy, and fertilize every two weeks with a liquid fertilizer. Overwinter the plant inside, or otherwise protect it in areas with freezing temperatures.

As the term is loosely and commonly used, "naturalizing" bulbs means planting bulbs that are adapted to one's local climate so that they will reproduce themselves and bloom year after year with little or no care. The term is also used to indicate random plantings in grasslands, woods, lawns, and like areas to imitate a natural setting. Keep in mind that if bulbs are to naturalize, their leaves must be left untrimmed to permit the plants to complete their cycle. Since this precludes mowing or cutting, allowances in one's garden plan must be made beforehand. Consider that for weeks, what had been a resplendent spring blanket of daffodils lining the drive will become a tangled mass of yellowing, dying leaves. Accordingly, planting later-flowering bulbs in front can disguise the less-sightly segment of nature's full cycle. ❧ If, after several years, the bloom of the naturalized bulbs appears to decline, it may be due to overcrowding, since they have continued to reproduce. In that case, after the leaves have withered and died, the bulbs should be lifted, separated, and replanted at a greater spacing.

AUTUMN CROCUSES

The colchicum bulbs, or autumn crocuses, as they are commonly called, are one of the few that flower in the fall, with their brilliant lavender and pink lily-shaped blooms making patches of pure color late into October. The flowers are born on pale, naked stems that break directly through the ground, unaccompanied by leaves of any kind. It is not until late winter or spring, well after the flowers are gone, that the long, strappy, sprawling leaves make a brief appearance and then die, unfortunately leaving a heap of yellowing, decaying leaves which you must leave in place for at least two months. ¶ The sight of autumn crocuses in full bloom, year after year, is perhaps worth the trouble of camouflaging the rather ungainly mass of leaves with flowers that grow and bloom in late spring and early summer. A good location for naturalizing would be one where the dead leaves of the autumn crocus would not be bothersome. ¶ The 'Water Lily' is an exceptionally beautiful variety of autumn crocus and will naturalize in all climates except those that are completely frost free. With a double layer of clustered, pointed petals, a group of these crocuses appears to be miniature waterlilies floating on the earth's dark surface. ¶ **HOW TO DO IT** ¶ For thirty bulbs, you will need 3 square feet of prepared ground in a location that receives a half-day or more of sun. Plant the bulbs 3 to 4 inches deep and 8 to 9 inches apart, and water thoroughly to saturate the soil. ¶ Allow leaves that appear in winter or spring to die back.

Autumn Crocus
Colchicum speciosum,
'Water Lily' and others

❧

8 inches tall
Pinkish lavender

❧

What You Need
30 bulbs
3 square feet of prepared ground
At least a half-day of full sun

❧

When to Buy
June through August from
mail-order catalogues
and nurseries

❧

When to Plant
June through August

❧

When Blooms Appear
1 to 2 months after planting

❧

DAFFODILS

Perhaps the easiest bulbs to naturalize are the virtually fail-proof daffodils. Because they are one of the earliest blooming of bulbs they can be planted under deciduous trees, where they can grow and bloom before the trees leaf out. ¶ As with the tulips, there are numerous classifications and varieties of daffodils, and many will naturalize successfully. Those with strong stems and sturdy blooms will withstand the buffeting of rain and wind better than those with less ample stems and more delicate flowers. 'Mount Hood' is a particularly sturdy white variety and in the bright yellow group a good beginner is the old standby, 'King Alfred.' ¶ To realize the glorious potential of sweeping plantings of naturalized daffodils, think in terms of planting bulbs by the bucketfuls, not handfuls. For a successful planting under a tree, count on using fifty bulbs or more. ¶ **HOW TO DO IT** ¶ For fifty bulbs, you will need a 4-foot square area of prepared ground in a sunny location. Plant the bulbs 7 inches deep, root sides down and points upward, 2 to 4 inches apart. The closer together they are planted the more solid the first year's bloom will appear. After planting, water thoroughly to saturate the soil. ¶ When the daffodils are through blooming, snap off any remaining flower heads and let the leaves grow until they wither and brown. The leaves then may be cut back or left to die. ¶ Fertilize in fall with a complete fertilizer.

Daffodil
Narcissus

❧

4 to 18 inches tall
Yellow, white, salmon, cream,
or bicolor

❧

What You Need
50 daffodil bulbs
4 square feet of prepared ground
A half-day or more of sun
Fertilizer

❧

When to Buy
August through November from
mail-order catalogues;
September through February
from nurseries

❧

When to Plant
September through February

❧

When Blooms Appear
Early to mid-spring

❧

MADONNA LILIES

Although many of the modern hybrid lilies are more fail proof, the romance of the Madonna lily's history should be ample to make you want to grow and naturalize it yourself. The Madonna lily appears in the annals of the Phoenicians and of ancient Greece and Rome, and it was planted in the cloister gardens of medieval monasteries, along castle walkways, and down through the centuries, until by the nineteenth century every self-respecting cottage garden had its "white lilies." The Madonna lily is deeply fragrant, and pure white with petals that gleam with a sheen of polished alabaster and fresh ivory. The yellow anthers, pollen-laden, will make orange smears if they brush against the white petals, so the flowers must be handled quite carefully. ¶ The 'Madonna' lily, not to be confused with the also white 'Easter' lily, is shallow rooted yet, unlike most other lilies, it thrives in full sun and dry, somewhat poor soil, as opposed to the rich soil that most of the other lilies must have. Excellent drainage is essential for success, so add extra sand to your soil if necessary. ¶ **HOW TO DO IT** ¶ For three bulbs, you will need 3 square feet of prepared ground. Dig a hole 8 inches deep and 8 inches wide for each bulb. Fill the hole a little over half-full with soil, and put one lily bulb in each hole, rounded root side down. Fill the holes with soil. The planted lily bulb should be no more than 1/2 inch deep. Water thoroughly to saturate the soil. In cold climates, cover with a mulch. ¶ Keep the ground moist throughout ✒

Madonna Lily

Lilium candidum

❧

5 feet tall

White

❧

What You Need

3 bulbs

3 square feet of prepared ground

Three-quarters to a full day of sun

Fertilizer

❧

When to Buy

May through early August from mail-order catalogues and nurseries

❧

When to Plant

August

❧

When Blooms Appear

10 months after planting, in early summer

❧

growth and bloom. Fertilize once a month. Once the bloom is over, snap off the blossom head but leave the stems, with their leaves, to wither and die, as these are the food source for the bulbs. ¶ Remember you are affecting next year's bloom when you cut blossoms to bring inside. However, if you take only a stem or two from each plant and cut it rather short, your lilies should survive. Another solution is to plant enough bulbs to both cut and naturalize.

Snowflakes

The most distinctive characteristic of this spring-blooming bulb is the green dot that appears on each white petal of the pendulant bell-shaped flower. Early-blooming snowflakes naturalize easily in rich, moist, slightly boggy soil. Planted near drain spouts, streambeds, or anywhere that they will receive lots of moisture they will rapidly multiply and spread. ¶ In nineteenth-century France, plantsmen had two quite different recommendations for gardeners concerning the planting of snowflakes. One was for gardeners to use snowflakes either alone or in combination with snowdrops, which also have a single green dot on each petal, or with early-blooming crocus to

make a naturalized geometric border around the gazon, or lawn. The other recommendation was completely the reverse — to scatter-plant snowflakes into the lawn, thus creating a natural, woodland look that would reappear each spring. ¶ Except in warm, dry climates, snowflakes are easy to grow and to naturalize. Moisture and rich soil are the essentials for success. ¶ There are two plants known as snowflakes, although they are quite different. The so-called summer snowflake has several bell-shaped flowers per stem, while the spring snowflake has only one large flower per stem. The summer snowflake will naturalize in most locations and does not need the moisture and rich soil that the spring snowflake does. ¶ **HOW TO DO IT** ¶ For fifty bulbs, you will need 10 square feet of prepared ground. Plant bulbs 4 inches deep and 4 inches apart. If you are planting into an existing lawn, dig single holes for each bulb. Water thoroughly to saturate the ground. ¶ Let the leaves wither and die before cutting them back. Fertilize in November before new growth occurs.

Snowflake

Leucojum vernum

18 inches tall

White

What You Need

50 bulbs

10 square feet of prepared ground

A quarter- to a half-day of full sun

Fertilizer

When to Buy

March through June from mail-order catalogues and nurseries

When to Plant

July through October

When Blooms Appear

5 to 6 months after planting, in spring

SPRING STAR FLOWERS

This little bulb naturalizes so readily that in some instances it may be found invasive, but it does have virtues that should be considered. It is one of the earliest flowers to bloom in spring, and because it is drought resistant once it has been planted it needs no further care at all. It is a wonderful choice to plant along the edges of rocky ravines or gullies or to tuck into stone walls or between the bricks of walkways, where the tiny blue-tinged white or sometimes blue flowers will appear spring after spring. ¶ Spring star flower is also called ipheion or Ipheion uniflorum and is most commonly sold under that name. ¶ **HOW TO DO IT** ¶ For fifteen bulbs you will need 1 square foot of prepared ground. Plant the bulbs 4 or 5 inches deep and about 2 inches apart, and water thoroughly to saturate the soil. ¶ After the leaves appear, let them wither and die back.

Spring Star Flower
Ipheion uniflorum
❧

6 to 10 inches tall
White, lavender, or blue
❧

What You Need
15 bulbs
1 square foot of prepared ground
At least a half-day of full sun
❧

When to Buy
June through November from mail-order catalogues and nurseries
❧

When to Plant
September through December
❧

When Blooms Appear
3 months after planting
❧

WILD TULIPS

Saxon Holt

Wild or "species" tulips, natives of the arid plateaus of ancient Anatolia, southern Russia, India, Persia, and southern Europe, have enthralled generations of tulip enthusiasts with their exotic origins, myriad shapes, varied colors, and different growing habits. For the most part they are early to bloom but small, ranging in height from 3 to 8 inches. The petals can be long, thin, and spiderlike, sharply pointed like waterlily petals, or rounded, reflexed, or fringed. Their colors encompass the spectrum. ¶ Happily, today a number of the species tulips are being commercially propagated and may be acquired with a little bit of astute searching. This is exciting for those of us who love the idea of naturalized tulips, planted in masses and clumps wherever there is room. The species tulips tend to naturalize in almost any climate except the very warmest, and will last years before their blooms begin to diminish and it is necessary to make new plantings. The hybrids of some of the species tulips are similar to the wild parents in garden performance — blooming early and with a tendency to naturalize — so they also are good choices for naturalizing. ¶ Although all tulips are striking when massed together, rather than as singletons here and there, this is especially true of the tiny species tulips. The more you can plant in a clump, border, or rock wall, the more dramatic they will be. It is important to plant them in an area where once they have bloomed they will be left alone, unwatered and untouched until the fall rains water them. ¶ Although there are many species tulips from which to choose, T. clusiana, a tallish red and white candy stripe, and T. batalinii, only 4 or 5 inches tall and creamy yellow, are two quite different types that are relatively easy to locate. ✏

Species Tulip

Tulipa clusiana, T. batalinii
and others
as well as their hybrids

❧

4 to 12 inches tall
Reds, pinks, whites, yellows,
or creams

❧

What You Need
48 bulbs
1-1/2 square feet of prepared ground
Full sun

❧

When to Buy
July through October from
mail-order catalogues, and
September through November from
specialty nurseries

❧

When to Plant
October through December

❧

When Blooms Appear
Early to mid-spring

❧

¶ **HOW TO DO IT** ¶ For forty-eight species tulip bulbs, you will need about 1-1/2 square feet of prepared, slightly moist, well-drained garden ground in a sunny location. Plant the bulbs about 8 inches deep and 1 to 2 inches apart. In most climates, rain and snow will provide adequate moisture, but you may want to water during the period of growth and bloom. After the tulips have bloomed, allow the leaves to wither and die back. Avoid watering during the summer.

Saxon Holt

BULBS TO

PLANT IN

GARDEN

BEDS

The choice of which bulbs to grow in your garden will often depend more upon your climate, growing conditions, and personal inclinations than upon the limitations of the bulbs themselves. In some instances bulbs may be planted directly in the ground and left there undisturbed to naturalize, while in other instances bulbs are planted with the realization that some extra care on the gardener's part will be needed to maintain them if they are to "regenerate" and flower again. ❧ Nonhardy bulbs with tropical or semitropical origins, such as dahlias, need to be protected in cold-winter areas by mulching or by being lifted and stored. Semihardy bulbs need to be lifted or mulched in areas with severe winters, while hardy bulbs grown in semitropical areas may need to be lifted and chilled before they will bloom again. ❧ In all instances, bulbs must be planted in garden soil that is light enough to provide good drainage. ❧ Regardless of whether or not you are leaving your bulbs in the ground or lifting them, you must allow the leaves to wither and die (in order to store energy) if the bulbs are to bloom successfully the following season. As with naturalizing, take into consideration how you will feel about browning foliage in your garden scheme.

AMARYLLIS

Amaryllis, the hippeastrum *hybrid, has* become associated so strongly with winter forcing that we tend to forget that these magnificent flowers of Amazonian ancestry can be grown in garden beds. ¶ Dozens and dozens of white, red, or salmon amaryllis flowers make an unforgettable sight grown casually along a garden walkway, when we are so used to seeing one stalk growing inside in solitary splendor. ¶ In Southern California and parts of Florida the bulbs can be left in the ground, where they will naturalize, but for the rest of us, the amaryllis must be treated as a one-time show or lifted and stored over winter. Even with care, success in cold climates is uncertain. ¶ **HOW TO DO IT** ¶ For a dozen bulbs, you will need a 10- to 12-square foot area of prepared ground in a sunny location. Plant the bulbs 8 inches deep, root sides down and points upward, 6 to 8 inches apart. After planting, water thoroughly to saturate the soil. ¶ Keep the soil moist but not soggy during growth and bloom. Fertilize after three weeks with a complete fertilizer. If you wish to keep the bulbs for another year, cut off the stems of the finished blooms. Continue watering until the foliage dies, then lift the bulbs and store them.

Hybrid Amaryllis

Hippeastrum hybrid

12 to 36 inches high

White, red, salmon, pink,
or variegated

What You Need

12 bulbs

10 to 12 square feet of prepared ground

At least three-quarters of a day of full sun

Fertilizer

When to Buy

June through January from
catalogues; late summer through early
spring from nurseries

When to Plant

September through December
in mild climates; after the last
hard freeze elsewhere

When Blooms Appear

Spring in mild climates;
summer elsewhere

Asiatic lilies

These spectacular star-shaped lilies bloom in clusters or singly and come in colors ranging from palest apricot to deep red. Some have lightly freckled throats, others appear brush-stroked with fine lines, and still others are splashed with color that fades and blends. There are flowers that face upward, downward, or outward. The flowers' petals may curl deeply or only slightly back toward the stem or be almost flat. The flowers are long lasting when cut, and unlike many lilies, may be cut on long stems without endangering the bulb's food storage capabilities. ¶ The Asiatic are notable for being easy to grow and will return to your garden year after year, as long as they are protected by mulching in winter. ¶ **HOW TO DO IT** ¶ For twelve bulbs you will need 6 square feet of prepared ground in a location that receives full sun all day in mild summers or a half-day of sun where summers are hot. For each bulb, dig a 10-inch deep hole and fill it three-quarters full with soil to which a complete fertilizer or well-rotted manure has been added. Place one bulb in each partially filled hole, root side down, and cover with soil. The bulbs should be no deeper than 2 inches below the surface. Water thoroughly after planting to saturate the soil. ¶ Keep the area moist throughout the growth and bloom of the lilies, and fertilize every two months with a complete fertilizer. If you want to overwinter the bulbs, continue to water even when the blooms are gone, then mulch, or lift the bulbs and store them.

Asiatic Lily

Lilium

❧

3 to 5 feet high

Reds, pinks, white, yellows, creams, or bicolor

❧

What You Need

12 bulbs

6 square feet of prepared ground

Full sun in mild summer areas; a half-day of sun in hot summer areas

❧

When to Buy

January through March from mail-order catalogues and nurseries

❧

When to Plant

September and October or March through May

❧

When Blooms Appear

June through July

❧

DAHLIAS

For huge, lush, foot-wide dahlia flowers bobbing on top of strong 4-foot stems, all the credit goes to the gardener. Unlike daffodils, which put on a spectacular spring show aided only by nature, the flamboyant, overblown, even garish giant dahlias need the gardener's guiding hand to succeed. ¶ The giant dahlias, and to a lesser degree the smaller ones, need staking and pruning. Staking protects the easily broken, brittle stems, and pruning allows the plant's resources to be allocated to a few blooms, rather than spread across many. However, as long as there is a minimum of support for your flowers, dahlias even unpruned will provide a magnificent display. ¶ The giant dahlias, as well as the small pom-pom, midsize cactus, and most of the other dahlias, are the result of intensive hybridizing during the past century or so for variations in color, petal shape, and size. Dahlias are now popular flowers in the florist industry, and their myriad forms are the subjects for avid garden collectors around the world. ¶ **HOW TO DO IT** ¶ For twelve giant dahlia bulbs, you will need 12 square feet of prepared ground in a sunny location. For each bulb, dig a hole 10 inches deep, then fill the hole just over half-full with a mixture of soil and dry complete fertilizer (according to package directions) or well-rotted manure (1 part to 2 parts soil). Drive a 5-foot-long stake a foot into the ground at the back of each hole. Now put the bulb or clump of bulbs in the hole with one "eye" of the bulb close to the stake. Fill the hole to the top with the remaining soil, and water until it is thoroughly saturated. ¶ You may want to make a 6-inch-deep ditch around each hole that you can later fill with water, to allow

Dahlia
Dahlia
❧
1 to 5 feet high
Reds, yellows, pinks, white, cream,
purple, or variegated
❧
What You Need
12 bulbs, giant flower type
12 square feet of prepared ground
At least three-quarters of a
day of full sun
Fertilizer
❧
When to Buy
January through March from mail-
order catalogues; January through April
from nurseries
❧
When to Plant
Spring in mild areas; early summer
elsewhere
❧
When Blooms Appear
2 to 3 months after planting
❧

gradual saturation of the soil around the growing plants. Fertilize once a month until bloom has finished. ¶ If you want a bushy appearance, when the plants are about a foot high pinch out the center stem, to force growth on the side branches. Gently tie the stalks to the stakes when the plants are 1-1/2 to 2 feet tall. For maximum, giant flower size, pinch off all but three or four stalks. Then, leaving only one bud at the end of each stalk, pinch off all the other buds. ¶ To keep the bulbs for the following season, lift and store them before the first hard frost. In temperate climates the bulbs may be left in the ground.

Early baby gladioli

Although these are essentially small versions of the tall, rigid flower spikes that are more commonly associated with florists than with home gardens, the miniature gladioli have some unique characteristics. *Their stems are more supple than the larger varieties' and their florets are generously spaced, giving the entire spike a more graceful appearance.* ¶ Like the dahlias, the modern garden gladioli are the result of extensive hybridization, of which the miniatures are but one example. *The miniatures alone are derived from more than five small-statured species types. One of them is gladiolus tristus, an unusual type which emits a sweet fragrance, but only at night. Large gladioli, like the small gladioli, flower all summer long and the bulbs, if heavily mulched, can be left in the ground over the winter.* ¶ **HOW TO DO IT** ¶ For twelve bulbs, you will need 2 to 3 square feet of prepared ground in a sunny location. Add a complete fertilizer and mix it into the ground. Plant the bulbs 4 inches deep, rounded root sides down, 2 to 3 inches apart. After planting, water thoroughly to saturate the soil. Keep the ground moist but not soggy throughout the life of the plant. ¶ In mild climates, the gladioli may be cut back after the foliage has died and then mulched over the winter. In other climates, they must be lifted and stored.

Gladiolus

Gladiolus, miniature types

❧

1 to 2 feet tall
White, pinks, reds, yellows, bicolor, or tricolor

❧

What You Need
12 bulbs
2 to 3 square feet of prepared ground
At least three-quarters of a day of full sun
Fertilizer

❧

When to Buy
January through April from mail-order catalogues and nurseries

❧

When to Plant
March through April, when all danger of frost is past

❧

When Blooms Appear
2-1/2 to 3 months after planting

❧

GIANT ALLIUMS

Ornamental alliums exist in a number of sizes, flowering patterns, and colors. An overwhelming specimen, the giant allium grows over 6 feet tall and has a spherical cluster of purple blossoms. The drumstick allium grows to five feet and produces clusters of dark purple blossoms tightly packed together to form a truncated oval. Drumsticks, like other giant alliums, are exceptional mixed into fresh bouquets with other summer flowers or used on their own. The decorative alliums also distinguish themselves as vertical elements in dry flower arrangements. They can be cut long on the stem and air-dried, either hanging or standing. If they are cut just as the buds begin to open, their colors will fare better, but if the blooms are allowed to open before cutting they will display their characteristic texture. ¶ Some varieties of alliums are quite small growing only five or six inches tall. These are good choices for rock gardens where they can be planted in among other small flowers and not lose their identity. ¶ The familiar kitchen onion and garlic are alliums as well, and when onion sets and garlic cloves are planted and left to flower, they produce spheres or umbrellas of tiny flowers atop long stalks very similar to those produced by ornamental alliums. ¶ As the plant approaches bloom, the allium stalks as well as the thick, tubular leaves often take on curvaceous shapes that can be as attractive and appealing as the flowers themselves. Flowering in early summer, the alliums create a subtle, muted picture in the garden that is in contrast to the sharp, clear colors of the summer-flowering dahlias and gladioli. ✦

Giant Allium

Allium giganteum

3 to 7 feet tall

Purple

What You Need

6 bulbs

3 square feet of prepared ground

A half-day or more of full sun

Fertilizer

When to Buy

*July through November from
mail-order catalogues;
September through December
from nurseries*

When to Plant

September through January

When Blooms Appear

Early to mid-summer

¶ HOW TO DO IT ¶ For six bulbs you will need 3 square feet of prepared ground that receives at least a half-day of sun. Plant the bulbs root sides down, tips upward, about 3 inches deep and 10 to 12 inches apart. Cover with soil, and water the ground thoroughly to saturate it. Keep the soil moist but not soggy, and fertilize about 10 days after the first shoots appear. **¶** After the bloom has finished, let the leaves wither and die before cutting them.

Exotic

Bulbs

Each of these exceptional bulbs has an element of charm that may be unfamiliar to the home gardener. The tuberose and the Peruvian daffodil are strongly fragrant.

Although you might have seen them in bridal bouquets or at a florist's and might even be familiar with their fragrance, growing them in your own garden is quite a different experience from receiving them across a counter, tightly rolled in florist's wrap. The bulbs for these exotic flowers, natives of Mexico and the highlands of the Andes, are actually quite readily available, and with a little extra care they can be grown successfully in most climates either in the ground or in containers, although they will naturalize only in mild climates. 🙟 The tall, elegant crinum is also fragrant. Although many crinum plantings still exist in old-time gardens, this bulb has unfortunately disappeared from the lists of most catalogue companies but can be located through diligent searching. 🙟 Petite size is the singular feature of the miniature daffodils, of which there are an increasing number of varieties available. Some of these are rare ones once only available in the wild. Please be sure to buy your bulbs from reputable dealers. There is an illegal trade in bare bulbs that is endangering the survival of some species. It is of gravest concern that we all only purchase bulbs from suppliers that are raising the bulbs themselves, not stealing them from the wild.

CRINUMS

From clumps of tropical-looking leaves, the summer-flowering crinum bulbs erect long, naked stalks that develop drooping clusters of pinkish trumpet-shaped flowers, which resemble the blooms of their relative, 'Pink Lady,' the belladona amaryllis. ¶ During the nineteenth and early twentieth century, crinums were popular garden borders in cottage and estate gardens in the southeastern United States and in those areas of Europe with a similar climate. Still today, driving through those regions in summer, you may well see huge edgings composed of the deep green, fleshy leaves, perhaps with flowers in bloom, especially in gardens that have not undergone modernization. ¶ Crinum were planted in the north as well, where they survived cold winters when they were provided with a heavy covering of mulch. In northern France, in the districts surrounding Paris, the crinum were protected from freezing temperatures by glass garden cloches. For added protection the bell-shaped cloches were filled with dead leaves, which further insulated the bulbs from the cold. Although there are many crinum, the two most commonly planted are Crinum bulbispermum, which has a reddish exterior with a pink or red interior and C. X powellii, which has white to rose-pink flowers. ¶ **HOW TO DO IT** ¶ For six bulbs, you will need 6 square feet of well-prepared ground in full sun. Plant the bulbs 5 to 6 inches deep and water thoroughly to saturate the soil. Keep it moist during growth and bloom, fertilizing plants monthly with a complete fertilizer. ¶ Let the leaves die back when the blooming period has finished and cover with mulch over the winter. Fertilize with a complete fertilizer in spring when the first new shoots appear.

Crinum

Crinum

❧

2 to 4 feet tall

Reddish, pink, or white

❧

What You Need

6 bulbs

6 square feet of prepared ground

At least a half-day of full sun

Fertilizer

❧

When to Buy

September through March from specialty mail-order catalogues and nurseries

❧

When to Plant

September through October in mild climates;

March through April after the last hard freeze in cold climates

❧

When Blooms Appear

Summer

❧

Miniature Daffodils

Like Lilliputians in a large-scale daffodil world, the small daffodils can be overwhelmed and their charm lost if they are mixed in with regular-size bulbs in a large garden planting. But for naturalizing in small gardens the miniatures are exceptionally well-suited, as well as for container plantings where each perfect detail of petal, cup shape, and coloration can be clearly seen and appreciated. ¶ Some of the miniature daffodils are species daffodils, such as Narcissus canaliculatus, which has clusters of tiny white blossoms with clear yellow cups and is only 6 to 8 inches tall, and the tiny and unusual 'Yellow Hoop Petticoat,' N. bulbodcodium conspicuus, only 5 inches tall with a flaring yellow skirt and narrow waist. Species daffodils used to be so extensively collected in the wild for sale that some were being threatened with extinction. However, bulb producers are now propagating the species types in their production fields, so along with the other types of daffodils, many of the species are commercially available. ¶ A number of hybrids have been bred from N. cyclamineus, a species characterized by petals that curl slightly and sweep back from ruffled cups. The small plants, 6 to 10 inches tall, in white, pale yellow, gold, and combinations thereof, are tiny replicas of the classic daffodil shape and are excellent to naturalize. They have names such as 'Peeping Tom,' 'Jack Snipe,' and 'Jenny,' and are readily available through mail-order catalogues. ¶ **HOW TO DO IT** ¶ For three to four miniature daffodil bulbs, choose a container 4 inches in diameter and 3 to 4 inches deep with a drainage hole in the bottom. Cover the bottom with a few pieces of gravel, pebbles, or bits of broken pottery. ¶ Fill the container with potting mix to within 2 inches of the rim. Place the bulbs on top of the potting mix, root sides down, pointed tips upward. Cover with mix to within 1/2 inch of the rim, and water thoroughly to saturate the potting mix. ¶ If you live in a cold climate, protect the potted bulbs during the winter by placing them inside in a ✦

Miniature Daffodils

Narcissus, dwarf species and hybrids

❧

4 to 10 inches tall

White, yellow, gold, or combinations

❧

What You Need

3 to 4 bulbs

Container at least 4 inches in diameter
and 3 to 4 inches deep

Gravel, small rocks, or bits of
broken pottery

Potting mix

¶

For Naturalizing

24 bulbs

2 square feet or a 6-foot border of
prepared ground

Location with at least a half-day
of full sun

Dry granular fertilizer

❧

When to Buy

July through November from
mail-order catalogues

❧

When to Plant

October through January

❧

When Blooms Appear

Early to mid-spring

❧

cool dark area until roots are developed and they show 2 inches of sprouts. Water them during this period, keeping the mix moist. Containers can then be moved to a protected location with bright light. In mild climates, containers can stay outdoors. Keep them moist during root development, growth, and bloom. If you wish to keep the bulbs for another growing season, let the leaves grow until they die back. ¶ For naturalizing, twenty-four to thirty-six miniature daffodil bulbs are enough for a 2-foot square area or a narrow 6-foot long border. Plant bulbs 2 inches apart and 5 inches deep in moist prepared garden soil in a location that receives a full or a half-day of sun. Cover with moist soil. ¶ After bloom, remove any remaining bloom heads and then stop watering and let the leaves yellow and die back.

PERUVIAN DAFFODILS

ooking like a botanist's dream of a cross between a daffodil and an orchid, spicily fragrant Peruvian daffodils masquerade under a variety of names. Sometimes they are called spider lilies, sea daffodils, and basket flowers, but all the names seem inadequate to properly describe the delicate white trumpet-shaped flowers. The gossamer blooms of white are almost transparent, with long, thin petals curling back from the seemingly torn edges of the blooms, away from the mesmerizing throat of apple green and bright gold. ¶ Elegant, graceful but fragile flowers, Peruvian lilies can be grown in most climates as long as a warm location and rich soil are supplied. They will bloom throughout the summer, but to bloom again the following year in all but the most temperate climates, they need to be protected over the winter by being lifted and stored. ¶ **HOW TO DO IT** ¶ For four Peruvian lily bulbs, choose a container 18 inches in diameter and 12 to 18 inches deep. Make sure the container has a drainage hole. Cover the bottom of the container with a layer of pebbles, gravel, or bits of broken pottery. With a mixture of one part sand, one part peat moss or other organic matter, and one part standard potting mix, fill to within 2 inches of the rim. Plant the bulbs, root sides down, pointed tips upward, on top of the mix. Cover with a 1-1/2-inch layer of the potting mixture and saturate it with water. ¶ Place the container in a warm, protected location in full sun. Keep the potting mixture moist, and fertilize once a month with a balanced fertilizer during growth and bloom.

Peruvian Daffodil
Hymenocallis narcissiflora

❧

18 inches to 2 feet tall
White or yellow

❧

What You Need
4 bulbs
Container 18 inches in diameter
and 12 to 18 inches deep
Sand
Potting mix
Peat moss
Fertilizer

❧

When to Buy
September through March

❧

When to Plant
September through March in
frost-free climates;
April or after the last frost in
cold climates

❧

When Blooms Appear
Summer

❧

TUBEROSES

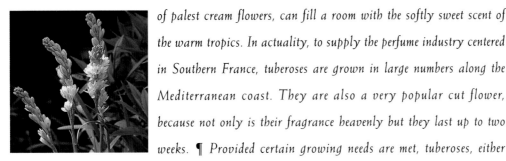

Tuberoses are so fragrant that just two or three of the long, blooming spears, each with rows of palest cream flowers, can fill a room with the softly sweet scent of the warm tropics. In actuality, to supply the perfume industry centered in Southern France, tuberoses are grown in large numbers along the Mediterranean coast. They are also a very popular cut flower, because not only is their fragrance heavenly but they last up to two weeks. ¶ Provided certain growing needs are met, tuberoses, either 'Mexican Single' or the double variety, 'The Pearl,' can be grown in most areas. They require a long growing season of warm weather — four months — to bloom, so in areas with a short growing season the bulbs should be started inside, then transplanted to the garden when the soil and air temperatures have warmed, typically in June. Tuberoses need a moist, rich, well-drained soil and a warm location. In colder areas, they can be planted, for example, against a south-facing wall to provide the most warmth possible. In areas with temperate climates, tuberoses can be planted directly in the garden as soon as the danger of frost has passed. ¶ **HOW TO DO IT** ¶ For six tuberose bulbs, you will need about a 2-foot square area. Plant the bulbs 8 inches apart and 2 inches deep, root side down, in prepared garden soil that has been enriched with organic matter. ¶ Cover the bulbs and water the soil until it is saturated. Keep the ground moist during the bulb's growing and blooming season and fertilize monthly. ¶ In the warm coastal areas of Florida and California, where temperatures do not drop to freezing, tuberoses will grow year-round, naturalizing in the garden. In other areas, it is necessary to lift and store the bulbs if you wish to replant them.

Tuberose

Polianthes tuberosa

❧

2 to 4 feet tall

Creamy white

❧

What You Need

6 bulbs

2 square feet of prepared soil

At least three-quarters of a day of full sun

Fertilizer

❧

When to Buy

October through March from mail-order catalogues and nurseries

❧

When to Plant

September through January in mild climates;

start inside in December through February in cold climates;

plant outside after the last frost

❧

When Blooms Appear

4 months after planting

❧

Further information on specific bulbs

AMERICAN BEGONIA SOCIETY
P.O. Box 471651
San Francisco, CA 94147
(707) 764-5407
www.begonias.org

AMERICAN DAHLIA SOCIETY
1 Rock Falls Court
Rockville, MD 20854
(301) 424-6641
www.dahlia.org

AMERICAN HORTICULTURAL SOCIETY
7931 East Boulevard Drive
Alexandria, VA 22308
(703) 768-5700
www.ahs.org

BRITISH GLADIOLUS SOCIETY
Frank Hartnell
Moors Edge, Athelney
Bridgewater, Summerset,
TA7 OSE, England

COMOX VALLEY DAHLIA SOCIETY
Jeanine Richardson
1686 Constitution Road
Black Creek, BC V9J 1G2
(250) 337-8985
www.dahlia.org

Sources

B & D LILIES
284566 US HWY 101
Port Townsend, WA 98368
(360) 765-4341
www.bdlilies.com

BRECK'S
P.O. Box 65
Guilford, IN 47022
(513) 354-1511
www.brecks.com

BRENT & BECKY'S BULBS
7900 Daffodil Lane
Glouchester, VA 23061
(877) 661-2852
www.brentandbeckys.com

CONNELL'S
10616 Waller Road East
Tacoma, WA 98446
(253) 531-0292
www.connells-dahlias.com

DUTCH GARDENS
128 Intervale Road
Burlington, Vermont 05401
(802) 660-3500
www.dutchgardens.com

MICHIGAN BULB COMPANY
P.O. Box 4180
Lawrenceburg, IN 47025
(513) 354-1497
www.michiganbulb.com

**GEORGE W. PARK
SEED COMPANY**
1 Parkton Avenue
Greenwood, SC 29647
(800) 213-0076
www.parkseed.com

**PEACEFUL VALLEY
FARM SPECIAL**
P.O. Box 2209
Grass Valley, CA 95945
(530) 272-4769
www.groworganic.com

JOHN SCHEEPERS, INC
23 Tulip Drive / P.O. Box 638
Bantam, CT 06750
(860) 567-0838
(860) 567-5323 Fax
www.johnscheepers.com

SPRINGHILL NURSERY
P.O. Box 330
Harrison, OH 45030
(513) 354-1509
www.springhillnursery.com

**K. VAN BOURGONDIEN
& SONS, INC.**
245 Route 109 / P.O. Box 1000
Babylon, NY 11702
(800) 552-9996
www.kvbwholesale.com

VESEYS
P.O. Box 9000
Charlottetown, PE, Canada
CIA 8K6
(902) 368-7333
www.veseys.com

WAYSIDE GARDENS
1 Garden Lane
Hodges, SC 29695
(800) 845-1124
www.waysidegardens.com

WHITE FLOWER FARM
P.O. Box 50, Route 63
Litchfield, CT 06759
(800) 503-9624
www.shepherdseeds.com

Peaceful Valley Farm Supply
P. O. Box 2209
Grass Valley, CA 95945
(916) 272-4769
(916) 272-4794 Fax
A wide selection of standard and unusual bulbs, with emphasis on easily grown varieties. Ships only in the fall.

Smith and Hawken Bulb Catalogue
25 Corte Madera
Mill Valley, CA 94941-1829
(415) 383-2000
Beautifully illustrated with color photographs, this catalogue has excellent horticultural information, a wide selection of unusual as well as standard bulbs, including many different lilies and species tulips.

John Sheepers, Inc.
P. O. Box 700
Bantam, CN 06750
(203) 567-0838
(203) 567-5323 Fax
A catalogue of unusual varieties of muscari, scillas, alliums, colchicums, species tulips, and miniature daffodils. The tulip selection is outstanding.

K. Van Bourgondien & Sons, Inc.
P. O. Box 1000
Babylon, NY 11702-0598
(800) 552-9996
(516) 669-1228 Fax
Large-quantity orders of both standard and unusual bulbs.

Van Engelen, Inc.
Stillbrook Farm
313 Maple Street
Litchfield, CT 06759
(203) 567-5662
Large-quantity orders of unusual and standard bulbs of all kinds.

Wayside Gardens
Hodges, SC 29695
(800) 845-1124
An all-purpose catalogue with a standard mix of bulbs. Find the Peruvian daffodil under the name Fragrant Sea Daffodil.

White Flower Farm
Litchfield, CT 06759
(800) 888-7756
(203) 496-1418 Fax
A wide selection of standard bulb varieties illustrated with color photographs. The lilies, daffodils, and tulips are outstanding.

BIBLIOGRAPHY

"Chez Un Collectionneur de Dahlias."
Elle Decor, no. 29.
March, 1992, p. 124.

Hortus Third Dictionary.
New York: Macmillan, 1976.

Larson, Roy A., editor.
Introduction to Floriculture.
Orlando, Florida: Academic Press, 1980

Leopold, Carl A.
Plant Growth and Development.
New York: McGraw- Hill, 1964.

Ortho.
All About Bulbs.
San Ramon, California:
Ortho Books, 1986.

Perenyi, Eleanor.
Green Thoughts.
New York: Vintage Books, 1983.

Scott, George Harmon
Bulbs, How to select, Grow and Enjoy
Los Angeles, California: HP Books, 1982

Sunset Western Garden Book.
Menlo Park, California:
Lane Publishing Company, 1978.

Vilmorin-Andreiux et Cie.
Les Fleurs de Pleine Terre.
Reprint of 1894 edition
by Les Editions 1900, 1989.

Weier, T. Elliot, et al.
Botany, fourth edition.
New York: John Wiley & Sons, Inc.,
1970.

Whiteside, Katherine.
Classic Bulbs.
New York: Villard Books, 1991.

Wister, Gertrude S.
Hardy Garden Bulbs.
New York: E. P. Dutton & Co., 1964.

INDEX

Acknowledgments

A very special thank you to Bill LeBlond and Caroline Herter, our editors at Chronicle Books, and Michael Carabetta, Chronicle Books' art director, for their unflinching enthusiasm and guidance as this book and its companion, *Little Herb Gardens* evolved. ¶ We also wish to thank Leslie Jonath at Chronicle Books for being there at all times when needed. ¶ Thank you to Carey Charlesworth, our editor, for her time and patience on the project and to Don Kinkead for working on the project at the 11th hour. ¶ Our enduring thanks to Jim Schrupp and Warren Roberts for the time and technical expertise they contributed to this book and to *Little Herb Gardens*. ¶ Thank you, Alta Tingle, Lynn Tingle, and the entire staff of The Gardener in Berkeley, California, for your generous contributions of ideas, time, and lovely wares. (see pages 8, 28, 36, 46) ¶ Thank you, Lisbeth and John Farmar-Bowers of Sonoma Flower Company and Skylark Nursery for the magnificent bouquets, cut flowers, gardens, and expertise you made available to us. (see pages 6, 32, 54, 55, 62, 63, 64, 65, 76, 77) ¶ We were very fortunate to have Michaele Thunen, floral stylist, work with us, and her resourcefulness and artistic flair were a great contribution. ¶ Thank you to the East Bay Nursery, Berkeley, California and to Whiting Nursery, St. Helena, California for allowing us to borrow plants and accessories. ¶ Finally, we wish to thank all of our friends, including A. Cort Sinnes, Charlotte Kimball, and Jill Cole whose gardening experiences have enriched our own, and the many professional horticulturalists who provide help and answers to us all. And a special thank you to Bruce LeFavour. ¶ An enthusiastic congratulations to Aufuldish & Warinner for giving our vision a beautiful reality.

We wish to thank all the generous and gracious people who opened their homes and gardens to us for photography.

❧

Mary Lu and Bob Schreiber
of Berkeley, California;
John and Lisbeth Farmar-Bowers
of Sonoma Flower Company/
Skylark Nursery,
Santa Rosa, California;
French Laundry Restaurant,
St. Helena, California
(see pages 18, 43);
Michaele Thunen
of Berkeley, California;
Susan Mills and family
of Berkeley, California;
Dr. Jay Vance
of Berkeley, California;
Carolee Luper
of St. Helena, California;
Sandra McHenry
of San Francisco, California;
Kathleen Stewart,
of Healdsburg, California;
St. Helena Antiques,
front cover pottery

❧